Bless Your Heart

A MOTHER'S JOURNAL

gift & paper expressions

...inspired by life

Bless Your Heart, A Mother's Journal
© 2008 Ellie Claire, Inc.
www.ellieclaire.com

Compiled by Joanie Garborg
Designed by Jeff & Lisa Franke for Lemon Lulu Studios, Minneapolis, MN

Scripture references are from the following sources: The Holy Bible, King James Version (KJV). The Holy Bible,
New International Version NIV. © 1973, 1978, 1984 by International Bible Society. The Message (MSG). © 1993, 1994,
1995, 1996, 2000, 2001, 2002 by Eugene Peterson. Used by permission of NavPress, Colorado Springs, CO. Used by
permission of Zondervan. The NEW AMERICAN STANDARD BIBLE (NASB), Copyright © The Lockman Foundation
1960, 1962, 1963, 1968, 1971, 1972, 1973, 1975, 1977, 1995. Used by permission. (www.Lockman.org). The Holy Bible,
New Living Translation (NLT) copyright © 1996 by permission of Tyndale House Publishers, Inc., Wheaton, IL.
www.newlivingtranslation.com. The New Revised Standard Version of the Bible: Anglicized Edition (NRSV), © 1989, 1995.
Division of Christian Education of the National Council of the Churches of Christ in the United States of America. Used by permission.
The Living Bible (TLB) © 1971. Used by permission of Tyndale House Publishers, Inc. Wheaton, Ill., 60189. All rights reserved.

Excluding Scripture verses, references to men and masculine pronouns have been replaced with gender-neutral references.

ISBN 978-1-934770-06-1
Printed in China

A MOTHER'S JOURNAL

WHAT IS A HOME?

What is home? A roof to keep out the rain? Four walls to keep out
the wind? Floors to keep out the cold? Yes, but home is more than that.
It is the laugh of a baby, the song of a mother, the strength of a father,
warmth of loving hearts, lights from happy eyes, kindness, loyalty, comradeship.
Home is first school and first church for young ones, where they learn
what is right, what is good, and what is kind, where they go for comfort
when they are hurt or sick; where joy is shared and sorrow eased;
where fathers and mothers are respected and loved, where children are wanted;
where the simplest food is good enough for kings because it is earned;
where money is not as important as loving-kindness; where even the tea kettle
sings from happiness. That is home. God bless it!

The godly walk with integrity; blessed are their children after them.

PROVERBS 20:7 NLT

WHAT IS A HOME?

CHILDREN'S CHILDREN

In ages past you laid the foundation of the earth, and the heavens
are the work of your hands. Even they will perish, but you remain
forever; they will wear out like old clothing. You will change them
like a garment, and they will fade away. But you are always the same;
your years never end. The children of your people will live in security.
Their children's children will thrive in your presence.

Psalm 102:25–28 NLT

Oh, that their hearts would be inclined to fear me
and keep all my commands always, so that it might go well
with them and their children forever!

Deuteronomy 5:29 NLT

---

*The resource from which He gives is boundless, measureless,
unlimited, unending, abundant, almighty, and eternal.*

JACK HAYFORD

CHILDREN'S CHILDREN

A MASTERPIECE

A mother has the special gift of always speaking true.
A mother gets the praise or blame if skies be dark or blue.
A mother is a doctor, a joiner or a vet,
the jobs a mother cannot do have not been heard of yet.
A mother is a power all wise, a tyrant or a saint,
an oracle, a paragon, with smart ideas or quaint.
Whatever else she may be, a mother knows full well,
a house could never be a home without her charming spell.

A child's hand in yours—what tenderness and power it arouses.
You are instantly the very touchstone of wisdom and strength.

Marjorie Holmes

A mother is not a person; she's a miracle.

Mary Hollingsworth

*T*he loveliest masterpiece of the heart of God is the heart of a mother.

Thérèse of Lisieux

Her children arise up, and call her blessed.

PROVERBS 31:28 KJV

A MASTERPIECE

THE BLESSING OF THE LORD

The Lord bless thee, and keep thee: the Lord make his face
shine upon thee, and be gracious unto thee: the Lord lift up
his countenance upon thee, and give thee peace.

Numbers 6:24–26 KJV

Let the loveliness of our Lord, our God, rest on us,
confirming the work that we do.
Oh, yes. Affirm the work that we do!

Psalm 90:17 MSG

How blessed is everyone who fears the Lord,
who walks in His ways.

Psalm 128:1 NASB

God bless you and utterly satisfy your heart...with himself.

AMY CARMICHAEL

THE BLESSING OF
THE LORD

SPECIAL GIFTS

Every person ever created is so special that their presence
in the world makes it richer and fuller and more wonderful
than it could ever have been without them.

We were not sent into this world to do anything
into which we cannot put our hearts.

John Ruskin

Use what talents you possess: the woods would be very silent
if no birds sang there except those that sang best.

Henry van Dyke

God gives everyone a special gift and a special place to use it.

Where you are right now is God's place for you.
Live and obey and love and believe right there.

1 CORINTHIANS 7:17 MSG

SPECIAL GIFTS

A THOUSAND GENERATIONS

Know therefore that the Lord your God is God; he is the faithful God, keeping his covenant of love to a thousand generations of those who love him and keep his commands.

Deuteronomy 7:9 NIV

For the Lord is good; his mercy is everlasting; and his truth endureth to all generations.... Thy kingdom is an everlasting kingdom, and thy dominion endureth throughout all generations.

Psalm 100:5, 145:13 KJV

I will sing of the mercies of the Lord for ever: with my mouth will I make known thy faithfulness to all generations.

Psalm 89:1 KJV

In following our everlasting God, we touch the things that last forever.

A THOUSAND GENERATIONS

ONLY ONE MOTHER

Most of all the other beautiful things in life come by twos and threes,
by dozens and hundreds. Plenty of roses, stars, sunsets, rainbows,
brothers and sisters, aunts and cousins, comrades and friends—
but only one mother in the whole world.

Kate Douglas Wiggin

A mother is...one who can take the place of all others,
but whose place no one else can take.

G. Mermillod

A mother is a rare book of which but one copy is made.

It is our uniqueness that gives freshness and
vitality to a relationship.

James Dobson

So give your parents joy! May she who gave you birth be happy.

PROVERBS 23:25 NLT

ONLY ONE MOTHER

LOVE LIKE THAT

Watch what God does, and then you do it, like children who learn
proper behavior from their parents. Mostly what God does is love you.
Keep company with him and learn a life of love. Observe how Christ loved us.
His love was not cautious but extravagant. He didn't love in order to get
something from us but to give everything of himself to us. Love like that.

Ephesians 5:1–2 MSG

I pray that your love for each other will overflow more and more,
and that you will keep on growing in your knowledge and understanding.

Philippians 1:9 NLT

*Open your hearts to the love God instills.... God loves you tenderly.
What He gives you is not to be kept under lock and key, but to be shared.*

MOTHER TERESA

LOVE LIKE THAT

SOMEONE SPECIAL

*T*he Creator thinks enough of you to have sent Someone very special so that you might have life—abundantly, joyfully, completely, and victoriously.

*W*hen we love someone, we want to be with them, and we view their love for us with great honor even if they are not a person of great status. For this reason—and not because of our great status—God values our love. So much, in fact, that He suffered greatly on our behalf.

John Chrysostom

*O*ne of Jesus' specialties is to make somebodies out of nobodies.

Henrietta Mears

God demonstrates His own love toward us, in that while we were yet sinners, Christ died for us.

ROMANS 5:8 NASB

SOMEONE SPECIAL

GOOD PLANS

Do not forget the things I have done throughout history. For I am God—
I alone! I am God, and there is no one else like me. Only I can tell you
what is going to happen even before it happens. Everything I plan
will come to pass, for I do whatever I wish.

Isaiah 46:9–10 NLT

"For I know the plans I have for you," declares the Lord, "plans to
prosper you and not to harm you, plans to give you hope and a future."

Jeremiah 29:11 NIV

No eye has seen, no ear has heard, no mind has conceived what
God has prepared for those who love him.

1 Corinthians 2:9 NIV

Every person's life is a fairy tale written by God's fingers.
HANS CHRISTIAN ANDERSEN

GOOD PLANS

SHE'S ALWAYS THERE

They might not need me;
but they might.
I'll let my head be just in sight;
A smile as small as mine might be
Precisely their necessity.

Emily Dickinson

Instant availability without continuous presence is probably
the best role a mother can play.

L. Bailyn

Mama's order was heavenly. It had to do with...taking plenty of time.
It had to do with taking plenty of time with me.

Susannah Lessard

To a child, love is spelled t-i-m-e.

Let the little children come to me, and do not hinder them,
for the kingdom of heaven belongs to such as these.

MATTHEW 19:14 NIV

SHE'S ALWAYS THERE

_____

_____

_____

_____

_____

_____

_____

_____

_____

_____

_____

_____

_____

_____

_____

_____

A RIVER OF DELIGHTS

*Y*our love, O Lord, reaches to the heavens, your faithfulness to the skies.
Your righteousness is like the mighty mountains, your justice like
the great deep.... How priceless is your unfailing love! Both high and low
among men find refuge in the shadow of your wings. They feast on the
abundance of your house; you give them drink from your river of delights.
For with you is the fountain of life; in your light we see light.

Psalm 36:5–9 NIV

God's love is like a river springing up in the Divine Substance and flowing endlessly
through His creation, filling all things with life and goodness and strength.

THOMAS MERTON

A RIVER OF DELIGHTS

GLORIOUS HANDIWORK

*H*e made you so you could share in His creation,
could love and laugh and know Him.

Ted Griffen

*Y*ou are a creation of God unequaled anywhere in
the universe.... Thank Him for yourself and then
for all the rest of His glorious handiwork.

Norman Vincent Peale

*T*he huge dome of the sky is of all things sensuously perceived the most
like infinity. When God made space and worlds that move in space, and clothed
our world with air, and gave us such eyes and such imaginations as those
we have, He knew what the sky would mean to us.... We cannot be certain that
this was not indeed one of the chief purposes for which Nature was created.

C. S. Lewis

The heavens declare his righteousness, and all the people see his glory.

PSALM 97:7 KJV

GLORIOUS HANDIWORK

DESIGNED ON PURPOSE

It's in Christ that we find out who we are and what we are living for.
Long before we first heard of Christ and got our hopes up, he had
his eye on us, had designs on us for glorious living, part of the
overall purpose he is working out in everything and everyone.

Ephesians 1:11–12 MSG

To every thing there is a season, and a time to every purpose
under the heaven.

Ecclesiastes 3:1 KJV

All the days ordained for me were written in your book
before one of them came to be.

Psalm 139:15-16 NIV

I delight to do thy will, O my God.

Psalm 40:8 KJV

*The patterns of our days are always rearranging...and each design for living
is unique, graced with its own special beauty.*

DESIGNED ON PURPOSE

_____

_____

_____

_____

_____

_____

_____

_____

_____

_____

_____

_____

_____

_____

_____

_____

JOYS OF HOME

*F*aces pressed at a window pane
Watching for someone to come again.
And I am the someone they want to see—
These are the joys life gives to me.
So let me come home at night and rest
With those who know I have done my best;
Let my [loved ones] rejoice and my children smile,
And know by their love that I'm worth while.
For this is conquest and world success—
A home where abideth happiness.

Edgar A. Guest

*H*ome is where there's one to love;
Home is where there's one to love us!

Roy Lessin

He settles the...woman in her home as a happy mother of children.

PSALM 113:9 NIV

JOYS OF HOME

_____

_____

_____

_____

_____

_____

_____

_____

_____

_____

_____

_____

_____

_____

_____

_____

_____

LAVISH GIFT-GIVING

How blessed is God! And what a blessing he is! He's the Father of our
Master, Jesus Christ, and takes us to the high places of blessing in him.
Long before he laid down earth's foundations, he had us in mind, had settled
on us as the focus of his love, to be made whole and holy by his love.
Long, long ago he decided to adopt us into his family through Jesus Christ.
(What pleasure he took in planning this!) He wanted us to enter into the
celebration of his lavish gift-giving by the hand of his beloved Son.

Ephesians 1:3–6 MSG

*Because of His boundless love, He became what we are
in order that He might make us what He is.*

IRENAEUS

LAVISH GIFT-GIVING

UNIQUE GIFTS

God has a wonderful plan for each person He has chosen. He knew even before He created this world what beauty He would bring forth from our lives.

Louis B. Wyly

Everyone has a unique role to fill in the world and is important in some respect. Everyone, including and perhaps especially you, is indispensable.

Nathaniel Hawthorne

God gives us all gifts, special abilities that we are entrusted with developing to help serve Him and serve others.

God has given gifts to each of you from his great variety of spiritual gifts... so that God's generosity can flow through you.

1 PETER 4:10 NLT

UNIQUE GIFTS

_____

_____

_____

_____

_____

_____

_____

_____

_____

_____

_____

_____

_____

_____

_____

_____

FAITH IS ...

*N*ow faith is being sure of what we hope for and certain of what
we do not see.... By faith we understand that the universe was formed
at God's command, so that what is seen was not made out of what
was visible.... And without faith it is impossible to please God,
because anyone who comes to him must believe that he exists
and that he rewards those who earnestly seek him.

Hebrews 11:1, 3, 6 NIV

*Faith, as the Bible defines it, is present-tense action. Faith means being sure of what we
hope for...now. It means knowing something is real, this moment, all around you, even when
you don't see it. Great faith isn't the ability to believe long and far into the misty future.
It's simply taking God at His word and taking the next step.*

JONI EARECKSON TADA

FAITH IS...

_____

_____

_____

_____

_____

_____

_____

_____

_____

_____

_____

_____

_____

_____

_____

_____

_____

GOD MADE HUGS

For my dear little child I'd lasso the moon
and give you my love on a silver spoon.
I'd run 'round the world and back again, too,
to grant you the hope of days bright and new.
But all that I have and all that I do
is nothing compared to God's love for you.

Everyone was meant to share
God's all-abiding love and care;
He saw that we would need to know
a way to let these feelings show....
So God made hugs.

Jill Wolf

Mother is the name for God in the lips and hearts of little children.

William Makepeace Thackeray

Love each other with genuine affection, and take delight in honoring each other.

ROMANS 12:10 NLT

GOD MADE HUGS

_____

_____

_____

_____

_____

_____

_____

_____

_____

_____

_____

_____

_____

_____

_____

_____

PATHS OF LIFE

But the path of the righteous is like the light of dawn,
that shines brighter and brighter until the full day.

Proverbs 4:18 NASB

You have made known to me the paths of life;
you will fill me with joy in your presence.

Acts 2:28 NIV

Thy word is a lamp unto my feet, and a light unto my path.

Psalm 119:105 KJV

Come, and let us go up to the mountain of the Lord...and he will
teach us of his ways, and we will walk in his paths.

Micah 4:2 KJV

*The best things are nearest...light in your eyes, flowers at your feet,
duties at your hand, the path of God just before you.*

ROBERT LOUIS STEVENSON

PATHS OF LIFE

WHAT MATTERS

The God who created, names, and numbers the stars in the heavens
also numbers the hairs of my head.... He pays attention to
very big things and to very small ones. What matters to me
matters to Him, and that changes my life.

Elisabeth Elliot

What matters supremely is not the fact that I know God, but the
larger fact which underlies it—the fact that He knows me. I am graven
on the palms of His hands. I am never out of His mind. All my knowledge
of Him depends on His sustained initiative in knowing me.
I know Him because He first knew me, and continues to know me.

J. I. Packer

One hundred years from today your present income will be inconsequential.
One hundred years from now it won't matter if you got that big break....
It will greatly matter that you knew God.

David Shibley

*I press on so that I may lay hold of that for which also
I was laid hold of by Christ Jesus.*

PHILIPPIANS 3:12 NASB

WHAT MATTERS

GOOD GIFTS

*E*very good gift and every perfect gift is from above,
and cometh down from the Father of lights, with whom
is no variableness, neither shadow of turning.

James 1:17 KJV

*R*ejoice in the Lord your God! For the rains he sends are
an expression of his grace. Once more the autumn rains will come,
as well as the rains of spring.

Joel 2:23 NLT

*H*e has not left himself without testimony: He has shown kindness
by giving you rain from heaven and crops in their seasons;
he provides you with plenty of food and fills your hearts with joy.

Acts 14:17–18 NIV

*All perfect gifts are from above and all our blessings show
The amplitude of God's dear love which any heart may know.*

LAURA LEE RANDALL

GOOD GIFTS

_____

_____

_____

_____

_____

_____

_____

_____

_____

_____

_____

_____

_____

_____

_____

_____

_____

_____

FAVORITE MEMORIES

The arrival of a new generation gives birth to the past, to the cycle of life,
the coming of each new season.... It brings a...panorama of childhood memories.

Doris Bryden Randall

There is nothing higher and stronger and more wholesome and useful
for life in later years than some good memory, especially a memory
connected with childhood, with home. Those who carry many such
memories with them into life are safe to the end of their days.

Fyodor Dostoevsky

Favorite people, favorite places,
favorite memories of the past...
These are the joys of a lifetime...
these are the things that last.

A family is a "gallery of memories" to those who have been
blessed by the presence of children.

James Dobson

To be in your children's memories tomorrow, you have to be in their lives today.

*Only the living can praise you as I do today. Each generation
can make known your faithfulness to the next.*

ISAIAH 38:19 NLT

FAVORITE MEMORIES

_____

_____

_____

_____

_____

_____

_____

_____

_____

_____

_____

_____

_____

_____

_____

_____

_____

_____

SHOW YOUR SPLENDOR

*S*atisfy us in the morning with your unfailing love,
that we may sing for joy and be glad all our days.
Make us glad for as many days as you have afflicted us,
for as many years as we have seen trouble.
May your deeds be shown to your servants,
your splendor to their children.
May the favor of the Lord our God rest upon us;
establish the work of our hands for us—
yes, establish the work of our hands.

Psalm 90:14–17 NIV

Today Jesus is working just as wonderful works as when He created the heaven and the earth.
His wondrous grace, His wonderful omnipotence, is for His child who trusts Him, even today.

CHARLES E. HURLBURT AND T. C. HORTON

SHOW YOUR SPLENDOR

ENDLESS WONDERS

Little drops of water,
Little grains of sand,
Make the mighty ocean
And the pleasant land.
Little deeds of kindness,
Little words of love,
Help to make earth happy
Like the heaven above.

Julia Fletcher Carney

As we grow in our capacities to see and enjoy the joys that
God has placed in our lives, life becomes a glorious experience
of discovering His endless wonders.

I will show wonders in the heavens and on the earth.

JOEL 2:28-30 NIV

ENDLESS WONDERS

FAITHFULNESS TO THE CLOUDS

For your unfailing love is as high as the heavens. Your faithfulness
reaches to the clouds. Be exalted, O God, above the highest heavens.
May your glory shine over all the earth.

Psalm 57:10–11 NLT

The deeper your love, the higher it goes; every cloud's
a flag to your faithfulness. Soar high in the skies, O God!
Cover the whole earth with your glory!

Psalm 108:4–5 MSG

Not to us, O Lord, not to us, but to Your name give glory
because of Your lovingkindness, because of Your truth.

Psalm 115:1 NASB

Be assured, if you walk with Him and look to Him and expect help from Him,
He will never fail you.

GEORGE MÜELLER

FAITHFULNESS TO
THE CLOUDS

_____

_____

_____

_____

_____

_____

_____

_____

_____

_____

_____

_____

_____

_____

_____

_____

_____

_____

WINGS OF LOVE

A child's spirit is like a child: you can never catch it by running after it;
you must stand still, and for love, it will soon itself come back.

Arthur Miller

You are the gate through which it came into the world,
and you will be allowed to have charge of it for a period;
after that it will leave you and blossom out into its own free life—
and there it is, for you to watch, living its life in freedom.

Agatha Christie

There are two lasting bequests we can give our children.
One of these is roots; the other, wings.

Hodding Carter

A mother's love gives us wings.

Use your freedom to serve one another in love; that's how freedom grows.

GALATIANS 5:13 MSG

WINGS OF LOVE

_____

_____

_____

_____

_____

_____

_____

_____

_____

_____

_____

_____

_____

_____

_____

_____

HIS GREAT POWER

Search high and low, scan skies and land, you'll find nothing and
no one quite like God. The holy angels are in awe before him;
he looms immense and august over everyone around him. God of the
Angel Armies, who is like you, powerful and faithful from every angle?

Psalm 89:6–8 MSG

Yours, O Lord, is the greatness and the power and the glory
and the majesty and the splendor, for everything in
heaven and earth is yours. Yours, O Lord, is the kingdom;
you are exalted as head over all.

1 Chronicles 29:11 NIV

Ah, Sovereign Lord, you have made the heavens and the earth by your
great power and outstretched arm. Nothing is too hard for you.

Jeremiah 32:17 NIV

Whatever the circumstances, whatever the call…
His strength will be your strength in your hour of need.

BILLY GRAHAM

HIS GREAT POWER

_____

_____

_____

_____

_____

_____

_____

_____

_____

_____

_____

_____

_____

_____

_____

_____

_____

_____

_____

MADE FOR JOY

Our hearts were made for joy. Our hearts were made to enjoy the One
who created them. Too deeply planted to be much affected by the ups
and downs of life, this joy is a knowing and a being known by our Creator.
He sets our hearts alight with radiant joy.

If one is joyful, it means that one is faithfully living for God, and that
nothing else counts; and if one gives joy to others one is doing God's work.
With joy without and joy within, all is well.

Janet Erskine Stuart

Live for today but hold your hands open to tomorrow. Anticipate the future
and its changes with joy. There is a seed of God's love in every event, every
circumstance, every unpleasant situation in which you may find yourself.

Barbara Johnson

The joy of the Lord is your strength.
NEHEMIAH 8:10 KJV

MADE FOR JOY

GOD DELIGHTS IN YOU

The Lord your God is with you, he is mighty to save.
He will take great delight in you, he will quiet you with his love,
he will rejoice over you with singing.

Zephaniah 3:17 NIV

You'll get a brand-new name straight from the mouth of God. You'll be
a stunning crown in the palm of God's hand, a jeweled gold cup held
high in the hand of your God. No more will anyone call you Rejected,
and your country will no more be called Ruined. You'll be called Hephzibah
(My Delight), and your land Beulah (Married), because God delights in you.

Isaiah 62:2–5 MSG

We are all precious in His sight.

GOD DELIGHTS IN YOU

_____

_____

_____

_____

_____

_____

_____

_____

_____

_____

_____

_____

_____

_____

_____

_____

_____

THE GARDEN OF LIFE

A garden of God is our childhood, each day
A festival radiant with laughter and play.

M. J. Lebensohn

*A*s the gardener is responsible for the produce of their garden,
so the family is responsible for the character and conduct of its children.

*M*others are the flowers in the garden of life.

*I*f I had a single flower for every time I think about you,
I could walk forever in my garden.

Claudia A. Grandi

You will be like a well-watered garden, like a spring whose waters never fail.

ISAIAH 58:11 NIV

THE GARDEN OF LIFE

REST IN HIM

*M*y soul finds rest in God alone; my salvation comes from him. He alone is
my rock and my salvation; he is my fortress, I will never be shaken.... My salvation
and my honor depend on God; he is my mighty rock, my refuge. Trust in him
at all times, O people; pour out your hearts to him, for God is our refuge....
One thing God has spoken, two things have I heard: that you, O God,
are strong, and that you, O Lord, are loving.

Psalm 62:1–2, 7–8, 11–12 NIV

*R*est in the Lord, and wait patiently for him.

Psalm 37:7 KJV

When God finds a soul that rests in Him and is not easily moved...
to this same soul He gives the joy of His presence.

CATHERINE OF GENOA

REST IN HIM

HAPPINESS AND GRATITUDE

It is not how much we have, but how much we enjoy, that makes happiness.

Charles H. Spurgeon

Sometimes our thoughts turn back toward a corner in a forest,
or the end of a bank, or an orchard powdered with flowers,
seen but a single time...yet remaining in our hearts and leaving
in soul and body an unappeased desire which is not to be forgotten,
a feeling we have just rubbed elbows with happiness.

Guy de Maupassant

Our inner happiness depends not on what we experience but on the
degree of our gratitude to God, whatever the experience.

Albert Schweitzer

I will bless the Lord at all times: his praise shall continually be in my mouth.

PSALM 34:1 KJV

HAPPINESS AND GRATITUDE

FREE TO LIVE

*G*od, your God, will cut away the thick calluses on your heart and
your children's hearts, freeing you to love God, your God, with your
whole heart and soul and live, really live.... And you will make a new start,
listening obediently to God, keeping all his commandments that I'm
commanding you today. God, your God, will outdo himself in making
things go well for you.... Love God, your God. Walk in his ways. Keep his
commandments, regulations, and rules so that you will live, really live,
live exuberantly, blessed by God.... Love God, your God, listening
obediently to him, firmly embracing him. Oh yes, he is life itself.

Deuteronomy 30:6–9, 16, 20 MSG

I asked God for all things that I might enjoy life.
He gave me life that I might enjoy all things.

FREE TO LIVE

_____

_____

_____

_____

_____

_____

_____

_____

_____

_____

_____

_____

_____

_____

_____

_____

_____

_____

THE BEST GIFTS

A mother knows the loving art of always giving with the heart.
She gives her children special things, like love and wisdom, roots and wings.

When she reviewed her parenting, she never thought...of the good school,
the advantages, as they were called. No, what she felt she had given them
was her attention: her love, her caring, her willingness to listen.

Marge Piercy

What will your children remember? Moments spent listening, talking,
playing, and sharing together may be the most important times of all.

Gloria Gaither

A mother is one who listens with her heart.

The gift of listening is one of the best gifts you can give your child,
any time of the year.

Come, my children, and listen to me, and I will teach you to fear the Lord.

PSALM 34:11 NLT

THE BEST GIFTS

FULL PROTECTION

But let all who take refuge in you be glad; let them ever sing for joy.
Spread your protection over them, that those who love your name
may rejoice in you. For surely, O Lord, you bless the righteous;
you surround them with your favor as with a shield.

Psalm 5:11–12 NIV

I will make my people strong with power from me! They will go wherever
they wish, and wherever they go, they will be under my personal care.

Zechariah 10:12 TLB

You have done so much for those who come to you for protection,
blessing them before the watching world.

Psalm 31:19 NLT

I am with you and will keep you wherever you go.

Genesis 28:15 NASB

*God is steadfast as your rock, faithful as your protector,
sleepless as your watcher.*

FULL PROTECTION

COMPLETELY LOVED

*W*hat good news! God knows us completely and still loves us.

*Y*ou are valuable just because you exist. Not because of what
you do or what you have done, but simply because you are.
Just think about the way Jesus honors you…and smile.

Max Lucado

*W*e are of such value to God that He came to live among us…
and to guide us home. He will go to any length to seek us….
We can only respond by loving God for His love.

Catherine of Siena

We love him, because he first loved us.

1 JOHN 4:19 KJV

COMPLETELY LOVED

JARS OF CLAY

But thanks be to God, who always leads us in triumphal procession
in Christ and through us spreads everywhere the fragrance of the
knowledge of him. For we are to God the aroma of Christ among
those who are being saved and those who are perishing.

2 Corinthians 2:14–15 NIV

For God, who said, "Let light shine out of darkness," made his light
shine in our hearts to give us the light of the knowledge of the glory of
God in the face of Christ. But we have this treasure in jars of clay to
show that this all-surpassing power is from God and not from us.

2 Corinthians 4:6–7 NIV

Lord, help me to spread Your fragrance everywhere I go,
and may Your radiant light be visible through me.

JARS OF CLAY

WATCHFUL CARE

*H*e paints the lily of the field,
Perfumes each lily bell;
If He so loves the little flowers,
I know He loves me well.

Maria Straus

*G*od cares for the world He created, from the rising of a nation to
the falling of the sparrow. Everything in the world lies under the watchful
gaze of His providential eyes, from the numbering of the days of our life
to the numbering of the hairs on our head. When we look at the world
from that perspective, it produces within us a response of reverence.

Ken Gire

*G*od's in His heaven—
All's right with the world!

Robert Browning

For He will give His angels charge concerning you, to guard you in all your ways.

PSALM 91:11 NASB

WATCHFUL CARE

WIDE OPEN SPACES

*B*y entering through faith into what God has always wanted to do
for us—set us right with him, make us fit for him—we have it all
together with God because of our Master Jesus. And that's not all:
We throw open our doors to God and discover at the same moment
that he has already thrown open his door to us. We find ourselves
standing where we always hoped we might stand—out in the wide open
spaces of God's grace and glory, standing tall and shouting our praise.

Romans 5:1–2 MSG

Whoever walks toward God one step, God runs toward him two.

WIDE OPEN SPACES

JOY AND DREAMS

A mother is someone who dreams great dreams for you, but then she lets
you chase the dreams you have for yourself and loves you just the same.
In the end, she believes in your dreams as much as you do.

*O*ne should take children's philosophy to heart. They do not despise a bubble
because it bursts. They immediately set to work to blow another one.

*A*llow children to be happy in their own way,
for what better way will they ever find?

Samuel Johnson

*W*hatever you do, put romance and enthusiasm into the lives of your children.

Margaret R. MacDonald

*C*hildren have neither past nor future; they enjoy the present,
which very few of us do.

Jean de la Bruyère

*You have set your glory above the heavens. From the lips of children
and infants you have ordained praise*

PSALM 8:1-2 NIV

JOY AND DREAMS

TENDER LOVE

For all God's words are right, and everything he does is worthy of our trust.
He loves whatever is just and good; the earth is filled with his tender love.

Psalm 33:4–5 TLB

For, lo, the winter is past, the rain is over and gone; the flowers
appear on the earth; the time of the singing of birds is come.

Song of Solomon 2:11–12 KJV

He has remembered his love and his faithfulness...all the ends
of the earth have seen the salvation of our God.

Psalm 98:3 NIV

---

*Love is the sweet, tender, melting nature of God flowing into the creature,
making the creature most like unto himself.*

ISAAC PENNINGTON

TENDER LOVE

_____

_____

_____

_____

_____

_____

_____

_____

_____

_____

_____

_____

_____

_____

HOME SWEET HOME

"I'm going home." There may be sweeter phrases in the English language—
"I love you," for example. But few phrases pack as much emotional
wallop as the simple expression of returning to the place of one's birth,
or to the haven of a house well lived in.

Gary Bauer

Mom, as often as I come back to your door, your love meets me on
the threshold, and your serenity gives me comfort and peace.

Where we love is home,
Home that our feet may leave,
But not our hearts.

Oliver Wendell Holmes

The road home is never long.

He blesses the home of the righteous.

PROVERBS 3:33 NIV

HOME SWEET HOME

_____

_____

_____

_____

_____

_____

_____

_____

_____

_____

_____

_____

_____

_____

_____

_____

_____

BOUNDLESS STRENGTH

I ask...the God of our Master, Jesus Christ, the God of glory...
to make you intelligent and discerning in knowing him personally,
your eyes focused and clear, so that you can see exactly what it is he
is calling you to do, grasp the immensity of this glorious way of life
he has for Christians, oh, the utter extravagance of his work in us
who trust him—endless energy, boundless strength!

Ephesians 1:17–19 MSG

*T*he Lord is great, and greatly to be praised.... The Lord made the
heavens. Honour and majesty are before him: strength and beauty
are in his sanctuary.... Give unto the Lord glory and strength.
Give unto the Lord the glory due unto his name.

Psalm 96:4–8 KJV

Strength, rest, guidance, grace, help, sympathy, love—
all from God to us! What a list of blessings!

EVELYN STENBOCK

BOUNDLESS STRENGTH

TREASURE IN NATURE

If we are children of God, we have a tremendous treasure in nature
and will realize that it is holy and sacred. We will see God reaching out
to us in every wind that blows, every sunrise and sunset, every cloud
in the sky, every flower that blooms, and every leaf that fades.

Oswald Chambers

The longer I live, the more my mind dwells upon the beauty
and the wonder of the world.

John Burroughs

Look up at all the stars in the night sky and hear your Father saying,
"I carefully set each one in its place. Know that I love you more than these."
Sit by the lake's edge, listening to the water lapping the shore and hear
your Father gently calling you to that place near His heart.

The heavens are telling the glory of God; and the firmament proclaims his handiwork.

PSALM 19:1 NRSV

TREASURE IN NATURE

_____

_____

_____

_____

_____

_____

_____

_____

_____

_____

_____

_____

_____

_____

_____

_____

_____

_____

THE WORD OF GOD

*F*or as the rain cometh down, and the snow from heaven,
and returneth not thither, but watereth the earth, and maketh it
bring forth and bud, that it may give seed to the sower, and bread
to the eater: So shall my word be that goeth forth out of my mouth:
it shall not return unto me void, but it shall accomplish that
which I please, and it shall prosper in the thing whereto I sent it.

Isaiah 55:10–11 KJV

*N*ot one word has failed of all His good promise.

1 Kings 8:56 NASB

God is the God of promise. He keeps His word, even when that seems impossible.

COLIN URQUHART

THE WORD OF GOD

_____

_____

_____

_____

_____

_____

_____

_____

_____

_____

_____

_____

_____

_____

_____

_____

_____

_____

THE MOST IMPORTANT THING

Children are our most valuable natural resource.

Herbert Hoover

The trouble with cleaning the house is it gets dirty the next day anyway,
so skip a week if you have to. The children are the most important thing.

Barbara Bush

Our children are the only earthly possession we take with us to heaven.

Children need adults who can go for casual walks...and slow down
to look at pretty leaves and caterpillars...and answer questions
about God and the nature of the world as it is.

James Dobson

*These commandments that I give you today are to be upon your hearts. Impress them on your
children. Talk about them when you sit at home and when you walk along the road.*

DEUTERONOMY 6:6-7 NIV

THE MOST IMPORTANT THING

LOVE ONE ANOTHER

*C*lothe yourselves with compassion, kindness, humility, gentleness
and patience. Bear with each other and forgive whatever grievances you
may have against one another. Forgive as the Lord forgave you. And over all
these virtues put on love, which binds them all together in perfect unity.

Colossians 3:12–14 NIV

A new command I give you: Love one another.
As I have loved you, so you must love one another.

John 13:34 NIV

*M*ay God, who gives this patience and encouragement,
help you live in complete harmony with each other.

Romans 15:5 NLT

*In God's wisdom, He frequently chooses to meet our needs by showing His love
toward us through the hands and hearts of others.*

JACK HAYFORD

LOVE ONE ANOTHER

_____

_____

_____

_____

_____

_____

_____

_____

_____

_____

_____

_____

_____

_____

_____

_____

_____

_____

A LIFE WORTHWHILE

I wish you humor and a twinkle in the eye. I wish you glory and the strength to bear its burdens. I wish you sunshine on your path and storms to season your journey. I wish you peace—in the world in which you live and in the smallest corner of the heart where truth is kept. I wish you faith—to help define your living and your life. More I cannot wish you—except perhaps love—to make all the rest worthwhile.

Robert A. Ward

*W*hat makes life worthwhile is having a big enough objective, something which catches our imagination and lays hold of our allegiance.... What higher, more exalted, and more compelling goal can there be than to know God?

J. I. Packer

I consider everything a loss compared to the surpassing greatness of knowing Christ Jesus my Lord

PHILIPPIANS 3:8 NIV

A LIFE WORTHWHILE

EACH NEW CHANCE

*G*od made my life complete when
I placed all the pieces before him....
God rewrote the text of my life
when I opened the book of my heart to his eyes.

Psalm 18:20, 24 MSG

*N*ow the God of peace...make you perfect in every good work
to do his will, working in you that which is wellpleasing in his sight,
through Jesus Christ; to whom be glory for ever and ever. Amen.

Hebrews 13:20–21 KJV

God puts each fresh morning, each new chance of life,
into our hands as a gift.

EACH NEW CHANCE

_____

_____

_____

_____

_____

_____

_____

_____

_____

_____

_____

_____

_____

_____

_____

_____

_____

_____

A GIFT FROM GOD

A mother is a gift from God
that's blessed in every part...
born through love and loyalty...
conceived within the heart.

I thank God, my mother, for the blessing you are...for the joy of your
laughter...the comfort of your prayers...the warmth of your smile.

*A*fter the love of God, a mother's affection is
the greatest treasure here below.

A mother is...the best friend God ever gave.

Christian Bovee

"Honor your father and mother"—which is the first commandment with a promise—
"that it may go well with you and that you may enjoy long life on the earth."

EPHESIANS 6:2 NIV

A GIFT FROM GOD

_____

_____

_____

_____

_____

_____

_____

_____

_____

_____

_____

_____

_____

_____

_____

_____

_____

_____

_____

GO OUT IN JOY

*Y*ou'll go out in joy, you'll be led into a whole and complete life.
The mountains and hills will lead the parade,
bursting with song. All the trees of the forest
will join the procession, exuberant with applause.

Isaiah 55:12 MSG

*Y*ou have made known to me the path of life; you will fill me with joy
in your presence, with eternal pleasures at your right hand.

Psalm 16:11 NIV

*H*e will yet fill your mouth with laughter
and your lips with shouts of joy.

Job 8:21 NLT

Those who run in the path of God's commands have their hearts set free.

GO OUT IN JOY

_____

_____

_____

_____

_____

_____

_____

_____

_____

_____

_____

_____

_____

_____

_____

_____

_____

_____

LOVE ONE ANOTHER

*Y*ou who have received so much love share it with others. Love others
the way that God has loved you, with tenderness.

Mother Teresa

*L*et Jesus be in your heart,
Eternity in your spirit,
The world under your feet,
The will of God in your actions.
And let the love of God shine forth from you.

Catherine of Genoa

*E*very single act of love bears the imprint of God.

Dear friends, since God so loved us, we also ought to love one another....
If we love one another, God lives in us and his love is made complete in us.

1 JOHN 4:11–12 NIV

LOVE ONE ANOTHER

ETERNALLY PRESENT

As parents feel for their children, God feels for those who fear him.
He knows us inside and out, keeps in mind that we're made of mud.
Men and women don't live very long; like wildflowers they spring up and
blossom, but a storm snuffs them out just as quickly, leaving nothing to show
they were here. God's love, though, is ever and always, eternally present
to all who fear him, making everything right for them and their children
as they follow his Covenant ways and remember to do whatever he said.

Psalm 103:13–18 MSG

God may be invisible, but He's in touch. You may not be able to see Him, but He is in control.
And that includes all of life—past, present, future.

CHARLES R. SWINDOLL

ETERNALLY PRESENT

SIMPLE HAPPINESS

I hope my children look back on today,
And see a mom who had time to play.
There will be years for cleaning and cooking,
For children grow up while we're not looking.

My childhood home was the home of a woman with a genius for inventing
daily life, who found happiness in the simplest of gestures.

Laura Fronty

The most important thing she'd learned over the years was that there was
no way to be a perfect mother and a million ways to be a good one.

Jill Churchill

Whether we are poets or parents or teachers or artists or gardeners,
we must start where we are and use what we have. In the process of
creation and relationship, what seems mundane and trivial may show
itself to be holy, precious, part of a pattern.

Luci Shaw

Don't you see that children are God's best gift?
the fruit of the womb his generous legacy?

PSALM 127:3 MSG

SIMPLE HAPPINESS

_____

_____

_____

_____

_____

_____

_____

_____

_____

_____

_____

_____

_____

_____

_____

_____

WATER OF LIFE

For I will pour water on the thirsty land, and streams on
the dry ground; I will pour out my Spirit on your offspring,
and my blessing on your descendants. They will spring up like
grass in a meadow, like poplar trees by flowing streams.

Isaiah 44:3–4 NIV

The earth shall be filled with the knowledge of the glory of the Lord,
as the waters cover the sea.

Habakkuk 2:14 KJV

Is anyone thirsty? Come!
All who will, come and drink,
Drink freely of the Water of Life!

Revelation 22:17 MSG

*Jesus…has been waiting all along for us to bring our needy selves to Him
and receive from Him that eternal water.*

DORIS GAILEY

WATER OF LIFE

A SPLENDID GIFT

This bright, new day, complete with twenty-four hours of opportunities, choices, and attitudes comes with a perfectly matched set of 1440 minutes. This unique gift, this one day, cannot be exchanged, replaced or refunded. Handle with care. Make the most of it. There is only one to a customer!

You have a unique message to deliver, a unique song to sing, a unique act of love to bestow. This message, this song, and this act of love have been entrusted exclusively to the one and only you.

John Powell, S.J.

Live your life while you have it. Life is a splendid gift— there is nothing small about it.

Florence Nightingale

Isn't everything you have and everything you are sheer gifts from God?

1 CORINTHIANS 4:7 MSG

A SPLENDID GIFT

_____

_____

_____

_____

_____

_____

_____

_____

_____

_____

_____

_____

_____

_____

_____

_____

_____

GOD'S THOUGHTS

*Y*our thoughts—how rare, how beautiful! God, I'll never comprehend them!
I couldn't even begin to count them—any more than I could count the
sand of the sea. Oh, let me rise in the morning and live always with you!

Psalm 139:17–18 MSG

*T*he counsel of the Lord standeth for ever,
the thoughts of his heart to all generations.

Psalm 33:11 KJV

*H*ow great are your works, O Lord, how profound your thoughts!

Psalm 92:5 NIV

"*M*y thoughts are completely different from yours," says the Lord.
"And my ways are far beyond anything you could imagine. For just as
the heavens are higher than the earth, so are my ways higher than
your ways and my thoughts higher than your thoughts."

Isaiah 55:8–9 NLT

*Just when we least expect it, He intrudes into our neat and tidy notions
about who He is and how He works.*

JONI EARECKSON TADA

GOD'S THOUGHTS

NEVER TO BE OUTGROWN

*S*traggler into loving arms,
Young climber up of knees,
When I forget thy thousand ways,
Then life and all shall cease.

Mary Lamb

*C*hildren help us rediscover the joy, excitement,
and mystery of the world we live in.

A boy is a magical creature—you can lock him out of your workshop, but you can't
lock him out of your heart. A little girl is...innocence playing in the mud, beauty
standing on its head, and motherhood dragging a doll by the foot.

Alan Beck

*N*o one ever outgrows the need for a mother's love.

Janette Oke

We were as gentle among you as a mother feeding and caring for her own children.

1 THESSALONIANS 2:7 NLT

NEVER TO BE OUTGROWN

SHOWERS OF BLESSINGS

*B*less the Lord, O my soul: and all that is within me, bless his
holy name. Bless the Lord, O my soul, and forget not all his benefits:
Who forgiveth all thine iniquities; who healeth all thy diseases;
who redeemeth thy life from destruction; who crowneth thee
with lovingkindness and tender mercies; who satisfieth thy mouth
with good things; so that thy youth is renewed like the eagle's.

Psalm 103:1–5 KJV

I will send showers, showers of blessings,
which will come just when they are needed.

Ezekiel 34:26 NLT

*God, who is love—who is, if I may say it this way, made out of love—
simply cannot help but shed blessing on blessing upon us.*

HANNAH WHITALL SMITH

SHOWERS OF BLESSINGS

_____

_____

_____

_____

_____

_____

_____

_____

_____

_____

_____

_____

_____

_____

_____

_____

_____

_____

HOLD FAST YOUR DREAMS

Hold fast your dreams!
Within your heart
Keep one still, secret spot
Where dreams may go
And, sheltered so,
May thrive and grow...
O keep a place apart,
Within your heart,
For little dreams to go!

Louise Driscoll

Always stay connected to people and seek out things
that bring you joy. Dream with abandon. Pray confidently.

Barbara Johnson

When dreams come true, there is life and joy.

PROVERBS 13:12 NLT

HOLD FAST YOUR DREAMS

RENEWING WORD

You're my place of quiet retreat; I wait for your Word to renew me....
Therefore I lovingly embrace everything you say.

Psalm 119:114, 119 MSG

You have dealt well with Your servant, O Lord, according to Your word.
Teach me good discernment and knowledge, for I believe in Your
commandments. Before I was afflicted I went astray, but now I keep
Your word. You are good and do good; teach me Your statutes.

Psalm 119:65–68 NASB

All your words are true; all your righteous laws are eternal.

Psalm 119:160

*Be still, and in the quiet moments, listen to the voice of your heavenly Father.
His words can renew your spirit...no one knows you and your needs like He does.*

JANET L. WEAVER SMITH

RENEWING WORD

_____

_____

_____

_____

_____

_____

_____

_____

_____

_____

_____

_____

_____

_____

_____

_____

GREAT POTENTIAL

*O*ne of the best things in the world to be is a child; it requires
no experience, but needs some practice to be a good one.

Charles Dudley Warner

*T*he potential possibilities of any child are the most
intriguing and stimulating in all creation.

Ray L. Wilbur

A child has two jobs. One is just being a child.
The other is growing up to be an adult.

*I*n every child is planted the seed of a great future.

A child is a handful some of the time,
But a heart-full all of the time.

May the Lord richly bless both you and your children.
May you be blessed by the Lord, who made heaven and earth.

PSALM 115:14-15 NLT

GREAT POTENTIAL

AS GOOD AS HIS WORD

*N*ot one word of all the good words which the Lord your God
spoke concerning you has failed; all have been fulfilled for you,
not one of them has failed.

Joshua 23:14 NASB

*T*he fulfillment of God's promise depends entirely on trusting God
and his way, and then simply embracing him and what he does.
God's promise arrives as pure gift.

Romans 4:16 MSG

*Y*our promises have been thoroughly tested;
that is why I love them so much.

Psalm 119:140 NLT

We may...depend upon God's promises, for...He will be as good as His word.

MATTHEW HENRY

AS GOOD AS HIS WORD

_____

_____

_____

_____

_____

_____

_____

_____

_____

_____

_____

_____

_____

_____

_____

_____

_____

_____

SPECIAL PLANS

This is the real gift: you have been given the breath of life, designed with a unique, one-of-a-kind soul that exists forever—the way that you choose to live it doesn't change the fact that you've been given the gift of being now and forever. Priceless in value, you are handcrafted by God, who has a personal design and plan for each of us.

May God's love guide you through the special plans He has for your life.

Allow your dreams a place in your prayers and plans. God-given dreams can help you move into the future He is preparing for you.

The Lord will work out his plans for my life—for your faithful love,
O Lord, endures forever.

PSALM 138:8 NLT

SPECIAL PLANS

PERFECT PEACE

*B*e careful for nothing; but in every thing by prayer and
supplication with thanksgiving let your requests be made known
unto God. And the peace of God, which passeth all understanding,
shall keep your hearts and minds through Christ Jesus.

Philippians 4:6–7 KJV

*Y*ou will keep in perfect peace him whose mind is steadfast,
because he trusts in you. Trust in the Lord forever,
for the Lord, the Lord, is the Rock eternal.

Isaiah 26:3–4 NIV

*P*eace I leave with you, my peace I give unto you:
not as the world giveth, give I unto you.
Let not your heart be troubled, neither let it be afraid.

John 14:27 KJV

The God of peace gives perfect peace to those whose hearts are stayed upon Him.

CHARLES H. SPURGEON

PERFECT PEACE

A WARM SANCTUARY

I once asked one of my smaller children what he thought a home was and he replied, "It's a place where you come in out of the rain." The home should be a warm sanctuary from the storms of life for each member of the family. A haven of love and acceptance. Not only children, but parents need this security.

Gigi Graham Tchividjian

*H*ome is the one place in all this world where hearts are sure of each other.

Frederick W. Robertson

A happy home is more than a roof over your head— it's a foundation under your feet.

*Y*ou're a foundation builder.... What could be more important than helping to shape and mold others' lives?

Guy Rice Doud

It takes wisdom to build a house, and understanding to set it on a firm foundation.

PROVERBS 24:3 MSG

A WARM SANCTUARY

GOD SO LOVED

*F*or God so loved the world, that he gave his only begotten Son,
that whosoever believeth in him should not perish, but have
everlasting life. For God sent not his Son into the world to condemn
the world; but that the world through him might be saved.

John 3:16–17 KJV

*T*his is My commandment, that you love one another, just as I have loved you.
Greater love has no one than this, that one lay down his life for his friends.

John 15:12–13 NASB

*M*ay the Lord direct your hearts into the love of God.

2 Thessalonians 3:5 NASB

Love Him totally who gave himself totally for your love.

C L A R E   O F   A S S I S I

GOD SO LOVED

_____

_____

_____

_____

_____

_____

_____

_____

_____

_____

_____

_____

_____

_____

_____

_____

GOD HEARS

*N*o matter where we are, God can hear us from there!

*A*nd then a little laughing prayer
Came running up the sky,
Above the golden gutters, where
The sorry prayers go by.
It had no fear of anything,
But in that holy place
It found the very throne of God
And smiled up in His face.

Amy Carmichael

We can now come fearlessly into God's presence, assured of his glad welcome.

EPHESIANS 3:12 NLT

GOD HEARS

DELIGHT IN THE LORD

$\mathcal{D}$elight yourself in the Lord and he will give you the desires of
your heart. Commit your way to the Lord; trust in him
and he will do this: He will make your righteousness shine like
the dawn, the justice of your cause like the noonday sun.

Psalm 37:4–6 NIV

$\mathcal{S}$end forth your light and your truth, let them guide me;
let them bring me to your holy mountain, to the place where you dwell.
Then will I go to the altar of God, to God, my joy and my delight.

Psalm 43:3–4 NIV

Our fulfillment comes in knowing God's glory,
loving Him for it, and delighting in it.

DELIGHT IN THE LORD

_____

_____

_____

_____

_____

_____

_____

_____

_____

_____

_____

_____

_____

_____

_____

_____

_____

CHANGING SITUATIONS

*T*he entry of a child into any situation changes the whole situation.

Iris Murdoch

A child enters your home and makes so much noise you can hardly stand it—
then departs, leaving the house so quiet you think you'll go mad.

J. A. Holmes

*O*nce the children were in the house the air became more vivid and
more heated; every object in the house grew more alive.

Mary Gordon

*O*ther things may change us, but we start and end with the family.

Anthony Brandt

*W*e had a disappointing experience with our children—they all grew up.

Leslie Bonaventure

---

*Look at all those children! There they sit around your table as vigorous and healthy
as young olive trees. That is the Lord's reward for those who fear him.*

PSALM 128:3-4 NLT

CHANGING SITUATIONS

WONDERFUL LOVE

*S*how the wonder of your great love.... Keep me as the apple of your eye;
hide me in the shadow of your wings.

Psalm 17:7-8 NIV

*G*ive thanks to the Lord, for he is good! His faithful love endures forever.

Psalm 136:1 NLT

*T*he Lord is gracious and merciful, slow to anger and abounding in steadfast love.
The Lord is good to all, and his compassion is over all that he has made....
The Lord is faithful in all his words, and gracious in all his deeds.

Psalm 145:8-9, 13 NRSV

---

*Every one of us as human beings is known and loved by the Creator
apart from every other human on earth.*

JAMES DOBSON

WONDERFUL LOVE

A LIFE OF PURPOSE

Happiness is living by inner purpose, not by outer pressures.

David Augsberger

I believe that nothing that happens to me is meaningless, and that it is good for us all that it should be so, even if it runs counter to our own wishes. As I see it, I'm here for some purpose, and I only hope I may fulfill it.

Dietrich Bonhoeffer

The meaning of earthly existence lies, not as we have grown used to thinking, in prospering, but in the development of the soul.

Aleksandr Solzhenitsyn

And we know that all things work together for good to them that love God, to them who are the called according to his purpose.

ROMANS 8:28 KJV

A LIFE OF PURPOSE

THE RIGHT WORD

*L*ike apples of gold in settings of silver is a word spoken in right
circumstances. Like an earring of gold and an ornament of fine gold
is a wise reprover to a listening ear. Like the cold of snow in the time
of harvest is a faithful messenger to those who send him.

Proverbs 25:11–13 NASB

*L*et everything you say be good and helpful, so that your words
will be an encouragement to those who hear them.

Ephesians 4:29 NLT

*W*hatever you do, whether in word or deed, do it all in the name of
the Lord Jesus, giving thanks to God the Father through him.

Colossians 3:17 NIV

Walk softly. Speak tenderly. Love fervently.

THE RIGHT WORD

THE BUILDER OF HOMES

The beauty of a house is harmony.
The security of a house is loyalty.
The joy of a house is love.
The plenty of a house is children.
The rule of a house is service.
The comfort of a house is in contented spirits.
The maker of a house, of a real human home, is God Himself,
the same who made the stars and built the world.

Frank Crane

May God, the best builder of homes and maker of families,
combine your hearts as one and unite you with never-ending love.

Every house has a builder, but the Builder behind them all is God.

HEBREWS 3:4 MSG

THE BUILDER OF HOMES

_____

_____

_____

_____

_____

_____

_____

_____

_____

_____

_____

_____

_____

_____

_____

_____

_____

_____

_____

A PERSONAL GUIDE

*B*ut I'll take the hand of those who don't know the way, who can't see where they're going. I'll be a personal guide to them, directing them through unknown country. I'll be right there to show them what roads to take, make sure they don't fall into the ditch. These are the things I'll be doing for them—sticking with them, not leaving them for a minute.

Isaiah 42:16 MSG

*W*hether you turn to the right or to the left, your ears will hear a voice behind you, saying, "This is the way; walk in it."

Isaiah 30:21 NIV

*W*e can make our plans, but the Lord determines our steps.

Proverbs 16:9 NLT

We have ample evidence that the Lord is able to guide. The promises cover every imaginable situation. All we need to do is to take the hand He stretches out.

ELISABETH ELLIOT

A PERSONAL GUIDE

NEW EVERY MORNING

*M*orning has broken like the first morning,
Blackbird has spoken like the first bird....
Praise with elation, praise every morning,
God's re-creation of the new day!

Eleanor Farjeon

*A*lways new. Always exciting. Always full of promise.
The mornings of our lives, each a personal daily miracle!

Gloria Gaither

*T*hat is God's call to us—simply to be people who are content
to live close to Him and to renew the kind of life in which
the closeness is felt and experienced.

Thomas Merton

*The steadfast love of the Lord never ceases, his mercies never come to an end;
they are new every morning; great is your faithfulness.*

LAMENTATIONS 3:22-23 NRSV

NEW EVERY MORNING

THE NEXT GENERATION

O my people, hear my teaching;
listen to the words of my mouth.
I will open my mouth in parables,
I will utter hidden things, things from of old—
what we have heard and known,
what our fathers have told us.
We will not hide them from their children;
we will tell the next generation
the praiseworthy deeds of the Lord,
his power, and the wonders he has done...
which he commanded our forefathers
to teach their children,
so the next would know them,
even the children yet to be born,
and they in turn would tell their children.
Then they would put their trust in God
and would not forget his deeds
but would keep his commands.

Psalm 78:1–7 NIV

---

*Teach your children why you believe what you believe.... Don't be afraid to teach them
to think for themselves. God's Word can withstand the test.*

PAUL MEIER

THE NEXT GENERATION

I'D RATHER BE A MOTHER

I'd rather be a mother
than anyone on earth
Bringing up a child or two
of unpretentious birth....
I'd rather wash a smudgy face
with round, bright baby eyes—
Than paint the pageantry of fame,
or walk among the wise.

A mother is neither cocky, nor proud, because she knows
the school principal may call at any minute to report that her child
had just driven a motorcycle through the gymnasium.

Mary Kay Blakely

A mother is one who knows you as you really are,
understands where you've been, accepts who you've become,
and still gently invites you to grow.

*Anyone who welcomes a little child like this on my behalf welcomes me,
and anyone who welcomes me welcomes my Father who sent me.*

MARK 9:37 NLT

I'D RATHER BE A MOTHER

BLESSINGS

*Y*ou're blessed when you're content with just who you are—
no more, no less. That's the moment you find yourselves
proud owners of everything that can't be bought.

Matthew 5:5 MSG

*B*lessed are those who hunger and thirst for righteousness,
for they shall be satisfied.

Matthew 5:6 NASB

*B*lessed are the merciful: for they shall obtain mercy. Blessed are
the pure in heart: for they shall see God. Blessed are the peacemakers:
for they shall be called the children of God.

Matthew 5:7–9 KJV

There is plenitude in God.... God is a vast reservoir of blessing who supplies us abundantly.

EUGENE PETERSON

BLESSINGS

SOURCE OF WONDER

I would maintain that thanks are the highest form of thought,
and that gratitude is happiness doubled by wonder.

G. K. Chesterton

*D*ear Lord, grant me the grace of wonder. Surprise me, amaze me,
awe me in every crevice of your universe.... Each day enrapture me
with Your marvelous things without number. I do not ask to see
the reason for it all; I ask only to share the wonder of it all.

Joshua Abraham Heschel

*M*ay our lives be illumined
by the steady radiance
renewed daily,
of a wonder,
the source of which
is beyond reason.

Dag Hammarskjöld

I will give thanks to the Lord with all my heart; I will tell of all Your wonders.
I will be glad and exult in You; I will sing praise to Your name, O Most High.

PSALM 9:1-2 NASB

SOURCE OF WONDER

GOD-PROVISION

*S*teep yourself in God-reality, God-initiative, God-provisions.
You'll find all your everyday human concerns will be met.
Don't be afraid of missing out. You're my dearest friends!
The Father wants to give you the very kingdom itself.

Luke 12:28 MSG

*Y*our Father knows that you need these things. But seek His kingdom,
and these things will be added to you. Do not be afraid, little flock,
for your Father has chosen gladly to give you the kingdom.

Luke 12:30–31 NASB

I am like a luxuriant fruit tree. Everything you need
is to be found in me.

Hosea 14:8 MSG

At the very heart of the universe is God's desire to give and to forgive.

GOD-PROVISION

PARENTING THEORIES

*B*efore I got married I had six theories about bringing up children;
now I have six children and no theories.

Lord Rochester

A characteristic of normal children is that they
don't act that way very often.

Franklin P. Jones

A little experience upsets a lot of theory.

*M*y personal theory is that God designed parenthood, in part,
as an enormous character-building exercise, and since God
does not personally require character improvement,
He didn't need to bother getting Adam to eat strained peas.

Dave Meurer

*Teach your children to choose the right path,
and when they are older, they will remain upon it.*

PROVERBS 22:6 NLT

PARENTING THEORIES

ROADS TO TRAVEL

If you want to live well, make sure you understand all of this. If you know what's good for you, you'll learn this inside and out. God's paths get you where you want to go. Right-living people walk them easily; wrong-living people are always tripping and stumbling.

Hosea 14:9 MSG

Enter through the narrow gate. For wide is the gate and broad is the road that leads to destruction, and many enter through it. But small is the gate and narrow the road that leads to life, and only a few find it.

Matthew 7:13 NIV

And how blessed all those in whom you live, whose lives become roads you travel; they wind through lonesome valleys, come upon brooks, discover cool springs and pools brimming with rain! God-traveled, these roads curve up the mountain, and at the last turn—Zion! God in full view!

Psalm 84:5-7 MSG

Heaven often seems distant and unknown, but if He who made the road... is our guide, we need not fear to lose the way.

HENRY VAN DYKE

ROADS TO TRAVEL

THE BEAUTY OF GOD'S PEACE

In comparison with this big world, the human heart is only a small thing. Though the world is so large, it is utterly unable to satisfy this tiny heart. Our ever growing soul and its capacities can be satisfied only in the infinite God. As water is restless until it reaches its level, so the soul has no peace until it rests in God.

Sadhu Sundar Singh

Peace is a margin of power around our daily need. Peace is a consciousness of springs too deep for earthly droughts to dry up.

Harry Emerson Fosdick

Drop Thy still dews of quietness
till all our strivings cease;
take from our souls the strain and stress,
and let our ordered lives confess
the beauty of Thy peace.

John Greenleaf Whittier

Be still, and know that I am God.

PSALM 46:10 KJV

THE BEAUTY OF
GOD'S PEACE

SEEN AND UNSEEN

*F*or the truth about God is known to them instinctively. God has put this knowledge in their hearts. From the time the world was created, people have seen the earth and sky and all that God made. They can clearly see his invisible qualities—his eternal power and divine nature. So they have no excuse whatsoever for not knowing God

Romans 1:19–20 NLT

*A*m I not present everywhere, whether seen or unseen?

Jeremiah 23:24 MSG

*S*o we fix our eyes not on what is seen, but on what is unseen. For what is seen is temporary, but what is unseen is eternal.

2 Corinthians 4:18 NIV

Live with eternity's values in view.

SEEN AND UNSEEN

FRESH INSIGHTS

With God, life is eternal—both in quality and length. There is no joy comparable to the joy of discovering something new from God, about God. If the continuing life is a life of joy, we will go on discovering, learning.

Eugenia Price

This life is not all. It is an "unfinished symphony"...with those who know that they are related to God and have felt the power of an endless life.

Henry Ward Beecher

Every day we live is a priceless gift of God, loaded with possibilities to learn something new, to gain fresh insights.

Dale Evans Rogers

So let us know, let us press on to know the Lord.... He will come to us like the rain, like the spring rain watering the earth.

HOSEA 6:3 NASB

FRESH INSIGHTS

THINK ON THESE THINGS

*W*hatsoever things are true, whatsoever things are honest,
whatsoever things are just, whatsoever things are pure,
whatsoever things are lovely, whatsoever things are of good report;
if there be any virtue, and if there be any praise, think on these things.

Philippians 4:8 KJV

*T*he Lord is in his holy Temple; the Lord still rules from heaven. He watches
everything closely, examining everyone on earth.... For the Lord is righteous,
and he loves justice. Those who do what is right will see his face.

Psalm 11:4, 7 NLT

*T*he fountain of beauty is the heart, and every generous
thought illustrates the walls of your chamber.

Francis Quarles

The happiness of your life depends upon the character of your thoughts.

THINK ON THESE THINGS

THEIR CHEERLEADER

If we can't keep up with our children, we can at least get behind them.

M. Scitter

A mother is a person with a sneaky knack
of saying good things about you behind your back.

A mother lifts your spirits and sticks with you when times are tough.
She stays by your side when everyone else has deserted you.

When you love someone, you love the whole person, just as he
or she is, and not as you would like them to be.

Leo Tolstoy

Though my children disappoint me a thousand times, I shall continue to
root for them...no matter how many mistakes they make.

Kel Grossclose

---

*Be humble and gentle. Be patient with each other,
making allowance for each other's faults because of your love.*

E PHESIANS 4:2 NLT

THEIR CHEERLEADER

_____

_____

_____

_____

_____

_____

_____

_____

_____

_____

_____

_____

_____

_____

_____

_____

THAT'S HOW MUCH
YOU MEAN

*D*on't be afraid, I've redeemed you. I've called your name. You're mine. When you're in over your head, I'll be there with you. When you're in rough waters, you will not go down. When you're between a rock and a hard place, it won't be a dead end—because I am God, your personal God, The Holy of Israel, your Savior. I paid a huge price for you...! That's how much you mean to me! That's how much I love you! I'd sell off the whole world to get you back, trade the creation just for you.

Isaiah 43:1–4 MSG

*I*f God be for us, who can be against us?

Romans 8:31 KJV

God is with us, and His power is around us.

CHARLES H. SPURGEON

THAT'S HOW MUCH
YOU MEAN

SHINING THROUGH

Don't ever let yourself get so busy that you miss those little but important extras in life—the beauty of a day...the smile of a friend...the serenity of a quiet moment alone. For it is often life's smallest pleasures and gentlest joys that make the biggest and most lasting difference.

Someone said to me once that we can see the features of God in a single smile. Look for that smile in the people you meet.

Christopher de Vinck

Dear Lord...shine through me, and be so in me that every soul I come in contact with may feel Your presence in my soul.... Let me thus praise You in the way You love best, by shining on those around me.

John Henry Newman

Nothing between us and God, our faces shining with the brightness of his face...our lives gradually becoming brighter and more beautiful as God enters our lives.

2 CORINTHIANS 3:18 MSG

SHINING THROUGH

WONDERFUL JOY

So be truly glad! There is wonderful joy ahead.... You love him even though you have never seen him. Though you do not see him, you trust him; and even now you are happy with a glorious, inexpressible joy.

1 Peter 1:6, 8–9 NLT

And the ransomed of the Lord will return. They will enter Zion with singing; everlasting joy will crown their heads. Gladness and joy will overtake them, and sorrow and sighing will flee away.

Isaiah 35:10 NIV

Rejoice evermore.

1 Thessalonians 5:16 KJV

*Through all eternity to Thee a joyful song I'll raise; for oh!
eternity's too short to utter all Thy praise.*

JOSEPH ADDISON

WONDERFUL JOY

A LOVING HOME

A mother's loving heart makes a loving home. Her love is the heart of the home. Her children's sense of security and self-worth are found there.

A mother is a person who if she is not there when you get home from school you wouldn't know how to get your dinner, and you wouldn't feel like eating it anyway.

She never quite leaves her children at home, even when she doesn't take them along.

Margaret Culkin Banning

I have seen many beautiful houses during my travels, but there is nothing that compares to one lavished with generations of love.

Mamie Thompson

Mid pleasures and palaces though we may roam,
Be it ever so humble,
There's no place like home.

John Howard Payne

I would lead you and bring you to my mother's house—she who has taught me.

SONG OF SONGS 8:2 NIV

A LOVING HOME

LOVE AND PRAYERS

*H*eavenly Father,
Thank You for the unique personalities that You have given to each and
every child. Help me to discover each talent and gift with which You
have blessed my children, and may I learn how to best cultivate each of
the blossoms You have planted within their souls. Amen.

Kim Boyce

*D*ear Lord, May my children grow to be confident, may they be healthy,
independent adults caring for themselves and reaching out to others. May they
have long, successful lives that grow from failures and errors I have allowed
them to make. May they have godly, helpful mates and satisfying careers.
Give me peace and contentment and when time marches on help me let them go.

Margaret Fishback Powers

*Finally, all of you should be of one mind, full of sympathy toward each other,
loving one another with tender hearts and humble minds.*

1 PETER 3:8 NLT

LOVE AND PRAYERS

_____

_____

_____

_____

_____

_____

_____

_____

_____

_____

_____

_____

_____

_____

_____

_____

_____

_____

_____

_____

_____

_____

_____

_____

_____

_____

_____

_____

_____

_____

> *Motherhood...is the only love I have known that is
> expansive and that could have stretched to contain
> with equal passion more than one object.*
>
> *Irma Kurtz*